Francis Frith's

Countryside

in Poetry and Prose

Chosen and edited by
Terence and Eliza Sackett

First published in the United Kingdom in 2004 by
Frith Book Company Ltd

Text and Design copyright © Frith Book Company Ltd
Photographs copyright © The Francis Frith Collection

The Frith photographs and the Frith logo are reproduced under licence from
Heritage Photographic Resources Ltd, the owners of the Frith archive and
trademarks.

British Library Cataloguing in Publication Data
Francis Frith's Countryside in Poetry and Prose
Chosen and edited by Terence and Eliza Sackett
ISBN 1-85937-938-9

Frith Book Company Ltd
Frith's Barn, Teffont,
Salisbury, Wiltshire SP3 5QP
Tel: +44 (0) 1722 716 376
Email: info@francisfrith.co.uk
www.francisfrith.co.uk

Printed and bound in Spain

Contents

The Earth is All Before Me

OH there is blessing in this gentle breeze,
A visitant that while it fans my cheek
Doth seem half-conscious of the joy it brings
From the green fields, and from yon azure sky.
Whate'er its mission, the soft breeze can come
To none more grateful than to me; escaped
From the vast city, where I long had pined
A discontented sojourner: now free,
Free as a bird to settle where I will.
What dwelling shall receive me? in what vale
Shall be my harbour? underneath what grove
Shall I take up my home? and what clear stream
Shall with its murmur lull me into rest?
The earth is all before me. With a heart
Joyous, nor scared at its own liberty,
I look about; and should the chosen guide
Be nothing better than a wandering cloud,
I cannot miss my way. I breathe again!
Trances of thought and mountings of the mind
Come fast upon me: it is shaken off,
That burthen of my own unnatural self,
The heavy weight of many a weary day
Not mine, and such as were not made for me …

WILLIAM WORDSWORTH (1770-1850)
from The Prelude Book 1

An Idler

I AM an Idler—as thorough and complete as any who ever went in debt for shoes to plod a vagrant journey through these threescore years and ten.

To plod—did I say? I have never plodded—never will plod.

I will follow where the whim leads, or drift like the thistle-down where the wind blows. Where the grass waves green, far from the dusty road; where the sparkling river hurls itself against boulders and dances between rocks in mad haste and passion to find the deep blue sea; where glossy beech trees spread across the woodland path to dapple bracken with a summer-mottled shade—these are the quiet haunts for my money …

The shining example of finest-quality, steam-rolled, double-twilled men of business, amidst whom my youth was spent, never once led me astray, nor induced me to dissipate in an orgy of money-making that energy for Idling which was Nature's choicest gift … For my own part, I would rather feel the crisp turf underfoot, and see the blue sky overhead, than spend my days within the four little walls of an office to earn the fee-simple of the earth … And if you do not look now, before the daylight is over—the opportunity is gone. There comes a cold wind—or a damp chill—or a microbe—and—

Oh no! No life amounts to anything whatever that is not three-parts energetic idling and industrious looking-about.

WALTER RAYMOND (1852-1931)
from The Idler Out of Doors

Return of Spring

NOW fades the last long streak of snow,
  Now burgeons every maze of quick
  About the flowering squares, and thick
By ashen roots the violets blow.

Now rings the woodland loud and long,
  The distance takes a lovelier hue,
  And drowned in yonder living blue
The lark becomes a sightless song.

Now dance the lights on lawn and lea,
  The flocks are whiter down the vale,
  And milkier every milky sail
On winding stream or distant sea;

Where now the seamew pipes, or dives
  In yonder greening gleam, and fly
  The happy birds, that change their sky
To build and brood; that live their lives

From land to land; and in my breast
  Spring wakens too; and my regret
  Becomes an April violet,
And buds and blossoms like the rest.

ALFRED, LORD TENNYSON (1809-1892)

Happy Families

LET any man observe, as I so frequently have with delight, the excessive fondness of the labouring people for their children. Let him observe·with what pride they dress them out on a Sunday, with means deducted from their own scanty meals. Let him observe the husband, who has toiled all the week like a horse, nursing the baby while the wife is preparing the bit of dinner. Let him observe them both abstaining from a sufficiency, lest the children should feel the pinchings of hunger. Let him observe, in short, the whole of their demeanour, the real mutual affection, evinced, not in words, but in unequivocal deeds … A labourer's cottage, on a Sunday; the husband or wife having a baby in arms, looking on two or three older ones playing between the flower-borders going from the wicket to the door, is, according to my taste, the most interesting object that eyes ever beheld …

WILLIAM COBBETT (1763-1835)
Advice to Young Men (and Incidentally to Young Women)

II

Chariot of the Sun

THE road skirts the marshland, the stream and the town, and goes through a gap in the Downs towards another range and more elms and farms at its feet. Stately walks the carter's boy with his perpendicular brass-bound whip, alongside four wagon-horses, while the carter rides. It is a pleasant thing to see them going to their work in the early gold of the morning, fresh, silent, their horses jingling, down the firm road. If they were leading their team to yoke them to the chariot of the sun they could not be more noble. They are the first men I have seen this morning, and truly they create for a little while the illusion that they are going to guide the world and that all will be well in the golden freshness under the blue.

EDWARD THOMAS (1878-1917)
from The South Country

Poor Old Horse

MY clothing was once of the linsey woolsey fine,
My tail it grew at length, my coat did likewise shine;
But now I'm growing old my beauty does decay,
My master frowns upon me; one day I heard him say,
  'Poor old horse, poor old horse!

Once I was kept in the stable snug and warm,
To keep my tender limbs from any cold or harm;
But now, in open fields, I'm forced for to go,
In all sorts of weather, let it be hail, rain, freeze, or snow.
  Poor old horse, poor old horse!

Once I was fed on the very best corn and hay
That ever grew in yon fields, or in yon meadows gay;
But now there's no such doing can I find at all,
I'm glad to pick the green sprouts that grow behind yon wall.
  Poor old horse, poor old horse!

'You are old, you are cold, you are deaf, dull, dumb and slow,
You are not fit for anything, or in my team to draw,
You have eaten all my hay, you have spoiled all my straw,
So hang him, whip him, stick him, to the huntsman let him go.
  Poor old horse, poor old horse!'

My hide unto the tanners then I would freely give,
My body to the hound dogs, I would rather die than live,
Likewise my poor old bones that have carried you many a mile,
Over hedges, ditches, brooks and bridges, likewise gates and stile.

    Poor old horse, poor old horse!

TRADITIONAL

A Wheelwright Buys his Timber

THE expeditions to buy oak were always in the late spring or the summer. The bark had been stripped then—it stood in big brown stacks beside the shining butter-coloured 'sticks' or butts of timber, where they lay in the brambles and newly springing fern. The 'lop and top'—the branches and twigs—had also been stacked, the bigger branches into cordwood, good for fires, the smaller—the twiggy boughs—into 'bavins' or 'sprays' such as bakers want for their ovens or potters for their kilns. So, the ground was clear enough for the wheelwright to examine his trees, and to measure them if he bought. And a delightful outing he had of it …

When the bargain was settled it remained to measure the timber—a pleasant and interesting job. To get the string between tree and ground (I never found a 'tape' measure of any use) I had a 'needle' or 'sword'—a slender and curved rod of iron—to push under the tree. At its end the needle was forged into a small hook like a button hook, and the looped string was then easily drawn back and so the circumference of the tree was taken. From that, to the 'girt', allowing for the thickness of the bark, and then (with slide-rule) calculating how many cubic feet of timber the tree held, was child's play. I liked it well, clambering over the prone tree-stems, amongst foxgloves and ferns perhaps. To guess the 'misure' of a tree, before actually taking its 'misure' —that in itself was a game. And, afterwards, the timber-carter liked to be told what the 'meetins' were—what was the average size of the trees he was sending his horses out to bring home.

GEORGE STURT (1863-1927)
from The Wheelwright's Shop

Getting a Waggon Together

ON recalling it I find myself wondering that a waggon was ever got together at all in my shop and under my management. Without pulleys or sling, strong arms alone had to raise the body from the ground and secure it to its two carriages; moreover, there needed to be a boy inside, to plunge the round-pin down into its place just at the critical moment – namely, when the pole from the hind-carriage was inserted into the fore-carriage and the body too was lying atop of them all right. Fewer than four men—to shift the wheels and so on—could hardly have done the necessary lifting—body and boy and all; and, as I was too ignorant, there was for the first months at any rate nobody to take command. Yet this seems not to have mattered. Waggons were constantly being 'taken down' for painting or mending, and then being lifted up again; and, as I remember no quarrel or disagreement over this work, I gladly believe that the workmen themselves liked to get it done efficiently and that their own friendly good temper taught them how to pull and lift together. Certainly it was an occasion for gruff jokes. Good humour saw us through. In one case, the round-pin having got jammed, a sledge hammer was called for to knock it down; whereupon the puny apprentice inside said 'Shan't I knock it down with my fist?' It's strange, how well I remember his smile after all these years.

GEORGE STURT (1863-1927)
from The Wheelwright's Shop

Home-Thoughts, from Abroad

O, TO be in England
Now that April's there!
And whoever wakes in England
Sees, some morning, unaware,
That the lowest boughs and the brushwood sheaf
Round the elm-tree bole are in tiny leaf,
While the chaffinch sings on the orchard bough
In England—now!

And after April, when May follows,
And the whitethroat builds, and all the swallows!
Hark, where my blossomed pear-tree in the hedge
Leans to the field and scatters on the clover
Blossoms and dewdrops—at the bent spray's edge—
That 's the wise thrush; he sings each song twice over,
Lest you should think he never could recapture
The first fine careless rapture!
And though the fields look rough with hoary dew,
All will be gay when noontide wakes anew
The buttercups, the little children's dower
—Far brighter than this gaudy melon flower!

ROBERT BROWNING (1812-1889)

Bluebells

9 May 1871. THE bluebells in the little wood … stood in blackish spreads or sheddings like the spots on a snake. The heads are then like thongs and solemn in grain and grape-colour. But in the clough/ through the light/ they came in falls of sky-colour washing the brows and slacks of the ground with vein-blue, thickening at the double, vertical themselves and the young grass and brake fern combed vertical, but the brake struck the upright of all this with light winged transomes. It was a lovely sight.—The bluebells in your hand baffle you with their inscape, made to every sense: if you draw your fingers through them they are lodged and struggle/ with a shock of wet heads; the long stalks rub and click and flatten to a fan on one another like your fingers themselves would when you passed the palms hard across one another, making a brittle rub and jostle like the noise of a hurdle strained by leaning against … The overhung necks—for growing they are little more than a staff with a simple crook but in water, where they stiffen, they take stronger turns, in the head like sheep-hooks or, when more waved throughout, like the waves riding through a whip that is being smacked—what with these overhung necks and what with the crisped ruffled bells dropping mostly on one side and the gloss these have at their footstalks they have an air of the knights at chess …

GERARD MANLEY HOPKINS (1844-1889)

The First Spring Day

I WONDER if the sap is stirring yet,
If wintry birds are dreaming of a mate,
If frozen snowdrops feel as yet the sun
And crocus fires are kindling one by one:
    Sing, robin, sing;
I still am sore in doubt concerning Spring.

I wonder if the springtide of this year
Will bring another Spring both lost and dear;
If heart and spirit will find out their Spring,
Or if the world alone will bud and sing:
    Sing, hope, to me;
Sweet notes, my hope, soft notes for memory.

The sap will surely quicken soon or late,
The tardiest bird will twitter to a mate;
So Spring must dawn again with warmth and bloom,
Or in this world, or in the world to come:
    Sing, voice of Spring,
Till I too blossom and rejoice and sing.

CHRISTINA ROSSETTI (1830-1894)

Prelude

PLEASANT it was, when woods were green,
    And winds were soft and low,
To lie amid some sylvan scene,
Where, the long drooping boughs between,
Shadows dark and sunlight sheen
    Alternate come and go;

Or where the denser grove receives
    No sunlight from above,
But the dark foliage interweaves
In one unbroken roof of leaves,
Underneath whose sloping eaves
    The shadows hardly move.

Beneath some patriarchal tree
    I lay upon the ground;
His hoary arms uplifted he,
And all the broad leaves over me
Clapped their little hands in glee,
    With one continuous sound;—

A slumberous sound—a sound that brings
    The feelings of a dream,—
As of innumerable wings,
As, when a bell no longer swings,
Faint the hollow murmur rings
    O'er meadow, lake, and stream.

And dreams of that which cannot die,
    Bright visions, came to me,
As lapped in thought I used to lie,
And gaze into the summer sky,
Where the sailing clouds went by,
    Like ships upon the sea.

HENRY WADSWORTH LONGFELLOW (1807-1882)

Binsey Poplars (felled 1879)

MY aspens dear, whose airy cages quelled,
Quelled or quenched in leaves the leaping sun,
All felled, felled, are all felled;
    Of a fresh and following folded rank
        Not spared, not one
        That dandled a sandalled
    Shadow that swam or sank
On meadow and river and wind-wandering weed-
    winding bank.

O if we but knew what we do
        When we delve or hew—
    Hack and rack the growing green!
     Since country is so tender
    To touch, her being so slender,
    That, like this sleek and seeing ball
    But a prick will make no eye at all,
    Where we, even where we mean
        To mend her we end her,
     When we hew or delve:
After-comers cannot guess the beauty been.
    Ten or twelve, only ten or twelve
      Strokes of havoc unselve
        The sweet especial scene,
      Rural scene, a rural scene,
      Sweet especial rural scene.

GERARD MANLEY HOPKINS (1844-1889)

Ploughman Singing

HERE morning in the ploughman's song is met
   Ere yet one footstep shows in all the sky,
And twilight in the east, a doubt as yet,
Shows not her sleeve of grey to know her by.
Woke early, I arose and thought that first
   In winter time of all the world was I.
The old owls might have hallooed if they durst,
   But joy just then was up and whistled by
A merry tune which I had known full long,
   But could not to my memory wake it back,
Until the ploughman changed it to the song.
   O happiness, how simple is thy track.
—Tinged like the willow shoots, the east's young brow
Glows red and finds thee singing at the plough.

JOHN CLARE (1793-1864)

Harry Ploughman

HARD as hurdle arms, with a broth of goldish flue
Breathed round; the rack of ribs; the scooped flank; lank
Rope-over thigh; knee-nave; and barrelled shank—
        Head and foot, shoulder and shank—
By a grey eye's heed steered well, one crew, fall to;
Stand at stress. Each limb's barrowy brawn, his thew
That onewhere curded, onewhere sucked or sank—
        Soared or sank—,
Though as a beechbole firm, finds his, as at a roll-call, rank
And features, in flesh, what deed he each must do—
        His sinew-service where do.

He leans to it, Harry bends, look. Back, elbow, and liquid waist
In him, all quail to the wallowing o' the plough: 's cheek
crimsons; curls
Wag or crossbridle, in a wind lifted, windlaced—
        See his wind- lilylocks- laced;
Churlsgrace, too, child of Amansstrength, how it hangs or hurls
Them—broad in bluff hide his frowning feet lashed! raced
With, along them, cragiron under the cold furls—
        With-a-fountain's shining-shot furls.

GERARD MANLEY HOPKINS (1844-1889)

The Sower's Song

NOW hands to seed-sheet, boys!
  We step and we cast; old Time's on wing,
And would ye partake of Harvest's joys,
  The corn must be sown in spring.
    Fall gently and still, good corn,
      Lie warm in thy earthy bed;
      And stand so yellow some morn,
        For beast and man must be fed.

Old Earth is a pleasure to see
  In sunshiny cloak of red and green;
The furrow lies fresh: this year will be
  As years that are past have been.
Fall gently …

  Old Earth, receive this corn,
    The son of six thousand golden sires:
All these on thy kindly breast were born;
  One more thy poor child requires.
Fall gently …

THOMAS CARLYLE/TRADITIONAL (19TH CENTURY)

On May Morning

NOW the bright morning-star, Day's harbinger,
Comes dancing from the East, and leads with her
The flowery May, who from her green lap throws
The yellow cowslip, and the pale primrose.
Hail bounteous May, that dost inspire
Mirth and youth, and warm desire
Woods and groves are of thy dressing,
Hill and dale doth boast thy blessing.
Thus we salute thee with our early song,
And welcome thee, and wish thee long.

JOHN MILTON (1608-1674)

Sheep Bells

'HOW many bells have you got on your sheep—it sounds as if you had a great many?' I asked of a shepherd the other day, feeding his flock near Old Sarum, and he replied, 'Just forty, and I wish there were eighty.' Twenty-five or thirty is a more usual number, but only because of their cost, for the shepherd has very little money for bells or anything else. Another told me that he had 'only thirty', but he intended getting more. The sound cheers him; it is not exactly monotonous, owing to the bells being of various sizes and also greatly varying in thickness, so that they produce different tones, from the sharp tinkle-tinkle of the smallest to the sonorous klonk-klonk of the big copper bell. Then, too, they are differently agitated, some quietly when the sheep are grazing with heads down, others rapidly as the animal walks or trots on; and there are little bursts or peals when a sheep shakes its head, all together producing a kind of rude harmony—a music which, like that of bagpipes or of chiming church-bells, heard from a distance, is akin to natural music and accords with rural scenes.

As to use, there is little or none. A shepherd will sometimes say, when questioned on the subject, that the bells tell him just where the flock is or in which direction they are travelling; but he knows better. The one who is not afraid to confess the simple truth of the matter to a stranger will tell you that he does not need the bells to tell him where the sheep are or in which direction they are grazing. His eyes are good enough for that. The bells are for his solace or pleasure alone. It may be that the sheep like the tinkling too—it is his belief that they do like it. A shepherd said to me a few days ago: 'It is lonesome with the flock on the downs; more so in cold, wet weather, when you perhaps don't see a person all day—on some days not even at a distance, much less to speak to. The bells keep us from feeling it too much. We know what we have them for, and the more we have the better we like it. They are company to us.'

W H HUDSON (1841-1922)
from A Shepherd's Life

A Painter's Delight

23 October 1821: HOW much I wish I had been with you on your fishing excursion in the New Forest! What river can it be? But the sound of water escaping from mill dams, willows, old rotten planks, flimsy posts and brickwork, I love such things. Shakespeare could make everything poetical; he tells us of poor Tom's haunts among 'sheep cotes and mills'. As long as I do paint, I shall never cease to paint such places. They have always been my delight, and I should indeed have been delighted in seeing what you describe, and in your company, 'in the company of a man to whom nature does not spread her volume in vain'. Still I should paint my own places best; painting is with me but another word for feeling, and I associate my 'careless boyhood' with all that lies on the banks of the Stour; those scenes made me a painter, and I am grateful; that is, I had often thought of pictures of them before I ever touched a pencil; but I will say no more, for I am a great egotist in whatever relates to painting.

JOHN CONSTABLE (1776-1837)
from a letter to Archdeacon Fisher

Fish for Dinner

NOW as an angler melancholy standing
Upon a green bank yielding room for landing,
A wriggling yellow worm thrust on his hook,
Now in the midst he throws, then in a nook.
Here pulls his line, there throws it in again,
Mendeth his cork and bait, but all in vain,
He long stands viewing of the curled stream;
At last a hungry pike, or well-grown bream
Snatch at the worm, and hasting fast away,
He knowing it a fish of stubborn sway,
Pulls up his rod, but soft, as having skill,
Wherewith the hook fast holds the fish's gill;
Then all his line he freely yieldeth him,
Whilst furiously all up and down doth swim
The ensnared fish, here on the top doth scud,
There underneath the banks, then in the mud,
And with his frantic fits so scares the shoal,
That each one takes his hide, or starting hole.
By this the pike, clean wearied, underneath
A willow lies, and pants (if fishes breathe)
Wherewith the angler gently pulls him to him,
And lest his haste might happen to undo him,
Lays down his rod, then takes his line in hand,

And by degrees getting the fish to land,
Walks to another pool: at length is winner
Of such a dish as serves him for his dinner …

WILLIAM BROWNE (1591-1645)
from Britannia's Pastorals

The Brook

… I wind about, and in and out,
  With here a blossom sailing,
And here and there a lusty trout,
  And here and there a grayling,

And here and there a foamy flake
  Upon me, as I travel
With many a silvery waterbreak
  Above the golden gravel,

And draw them all along, and flow
  To join the brimming river,
For men may come and men may go,
  But I go on for ever …

I slip, I slide, I gloom, I glance,
  Among my skimming swallows;
I make the netted sunbeam dance
  Against my sandy shallows …

And out again I curve and flow
  To join the brimming river,
For men may come and men may go,
  But I go on for ever.

ALFRED, LORD TENNYSON (1809-1892)

A Shepherd and the Stars

DETACHED hurdles thatched with straw were stuck into the ground at various scattered points, amid and under which the whitish forms of [Farmer Oak's] meek ewes moved and rustled. The ring of the sheep-bell, which had been silent during his absence, recommenced, in tones that had more mellowness than clearness, owing to an increasing growth of surrounding wool. This continued till Oak withdrew again from the flock. He returned to the hut, bringing in his arms a new-born lamb, consisting of four legs large enough for a full-grown sheep, united by an unimportant membrane about half the substance of the legs collectively, which constituted the animal's entire body just at present.

The little speck of life he placed on a wisp of hay before the small stove, where a can of milk was simmering. Oak extinguished the lantern by blowing into it and then pinching out the snuff, the cot being lighted by a candle suspended by a twisted wire. A rather hard couch, formed of a few corn sacks thrown carelessly down, covered half the floor of this little habitation, and here the young man stretched himself along, loosened his woollen cravat, and closed his eyes. In about the time a person unaccustomed to bodily labour would have decided upon which side to lie, Farmer Oak was asleep.

The inside of the hut, as it now presented itself, was cosy and alluring, and the scarlet handful of fire in addition to the candle, reflecting its own genial colour upon whatever it could reach, flung associations of enjoyment even over utensils and tools. In the corner stood the sheep-crook, and along a shelf at one side were ranged bottles and canisters of the simple preparations pertaining to ovine surgery and physic; spirits of wine, turpentine, tar, magnesia, ginger, and castor-oil being the chief. On a triangular shelf across the corner stood bread, bacon, cheese, and a cup for ale or cider, which was supplied from a flagon beneath. Beside the provisions lay the flute, whose notes had lately been called forth by the lonely watcher to beguile a tedious hour. The house was ventilated by two round holes, like the lights of a cabin, with wood slides.

The lamb, revived by the warmth, began to bleat, and the sound entered Gabriel's ears and brain with an instant meaning, as expected sounds will. Passing from the profoundest sleep to the most alert wakefulness with the same ease that had accompanied the reverse operation, he looked at his watch, found that the hour-hand had shifted again, put on his hat, took the lamb in his arms, and carried it into the darkness. After placing the little creature with its mother, he stood and carefully examined the sky, to ascertain the time of night from the altitudes of the stars.

The Dog-star and Aldebaran, pointing to the restless Pleiades, were half way up the Southern sky, and between them hung Orion, which gorgeous constellation never burnt more vividly than now, as it swung itself forth above the rim of the landscape. Castor and Pollux with their quiet shine were almost on the meridian: the barren and gloomy Square of Pegasus was creeping round to the north west; far away through the plantation, Vega sparkled like a lamp suspended amid the leafless trees, and Cassiopeia's chair stood daintily poised on the uppermost boughs.

'One o'clock,' said Gabriel.

THOMAS HARDY (1840-1928)
from Far From the Madding Crowd

Sheep Shearing

A BOY—the invariable boy who always appears upon these occasions—steals in delightedly to catch a ewe. As soon as they see him the whole flock rush about madly, as though they were executing a particularly confused set of kitchen lancers; but when once he has gripped one of them, after a few struggles she more or less resigns herself, and without any great resistance is half led, half dragged through the open hurdle to the malevolent-looking person who, like one of the Roman Fates, is waiting for her with the shears. He seizes her, and with an adroit and practised movement causes her to sit upon her tail, in which position most ewes look extraordinarily foolish. Now she struggles no more, nor does she make any noise; indeed, in watching the operations this morning I was put very forcibly in mind of the prophetic verse in Isaiah: 'As a sheep before her shearers is dumb'.

The operator begins his task in the region of the belly, working gradually round towards her back until it is necessary to turn the animal on to her side, when he ties the fore and hind leg together with a thin cord. In the case of old and experienced ewes I am sure that they understand what is happening to them, as they look quite contented and struggle little—indeed, the shearers say that this is so. The moment that the thing is done—which seems to prove it – they spring up with blitheness, and, rushing from the barn, begin to bite hungrily at the grass outside.

It is funny to watch the behaviour of the lambs that are waiting without. One by one they approach the escaped ewe, till at last its own offspring finds her. It takes a lamb a while, however, to convince itself that this strange, naked-looking creature is in truth its dear mamma; indeed, not until it has smelt her all round, and, thankful to find that something is left, knelt down, and with an air of relief helped itself to refreshment, does conviction conquer doubt.

RIDER HAGGARD (1856-1925)
from A Farmer's Year

Sunday Work

BETTESWORTH was 'huckin' about' in his garden when the curate passed by from church.

'He stopped an' he says, "Bettesworth, I wish this 'ere Sunday work was done away with altogether." I looked at 'n an' I says, "Well, sir," I says, "if it was, I dunno what in the world'd become o' you." He went off, an' my neighbour what was standin' near by says, "You fitted 'n that time, Freddy, 'bout as tight as ever I see." Well, and I was right. He only works Sundays.'

GEORGE BOURNE (1863-1927)
from The Bettesworth Book, 1901

Reckoning Age by the Thatch

THE oldest person in the village was a woman—as is often the case—reputed to be over a hundred: a tidy cottager, well tended, feeble in body, but brisk of tongue. She reckoned her own age by the thatch of the roof. It had been completely new thatched five times since she could recollect. The first time she was a great girl, grown up; her father had it thatched twice afterwards; her husband had it done the fourth time, and the fifth was three years ago. That made about a hundred years altogether.

The straw had lasted better lately, because there were now no great elm trees to drip, drip on it in wet weather. Cottagers are frequently really squatters, building on the waste land beside the highway close to the hedgerow, and consequently under the trees. This dripping on the roof is very bad for thatch. Straw is remarkably durable, even when exposed to the weather, if good in the first place and well laid on. It may be reckoned to last twenty years on an average, perhaps more. Five thatchings, then, made, eighty years; add three years since the last thatching; and the old lady supposed she was seventeen or eighteen at the first—that is, just a century since. But in all likelihood her recollections of the first thatching were confused and uncertain: she was perhaps eight or ten at the time, which would reduce her real age to a little over ninety.

RICHARD JEFFERIES (1848-1887)
from Wild Life in a Southern County

An Old Yorkshire Farmhouse

ONE step brought us into the family sitting-room, without any introductory lobby or passage: they call it here 'the house' pre-eminently. It includes kitchen and parlour, generally; but I believe at Wuthering Heights the kitchen is forced to retreat altogether into another quarter: at least I distinguished a chatter of tongues, and a clatter of culinary utensils, deep within; and I observed no signs of roasting, boiling, or baking, about the huge fireplace; nor any glitter of copper saucepans and tin cullenders on the walls. One end, indeed, reflected splendidly both light and heat from ranks of immense pewter dishes, interspersed with silver jugs and tankards, towering row after row, on a vast oak dresser, to the very roof. The latter had never been underdrawn: its entire anatomy lay bare to an inquiring eye, except where a frame of wood laden with oatcakes and clusters of legs of beef, mutton, and ham, concealed it. Above the chimney were sundry villainous old guns, and a couple of horse-pistols: and, by way of ornament, three gaudily painted canisters disposed along its ledge. The floor was of smooth, white stone; the chairs, high-backed, primitive structures, painted green: one or two heavy black ones lurking in the shade. In an arch under the dresser, reposed a huge, liver-coloured bitch pointer, surrounded by a swarm of squealing puppies; and other dogs haunted other recesses.

EMILY BRONTË (1818-1848)
from Wuthering Heights

Airs and Graces

WHEN the old farm-houses are down (and down they must come in time) what a miserable thing the country will be! Those that are now erected are mere painted shells, with a Mistress within, who is stuck up in a place she calls a parlour, with, if she have children, the 'young ladies and gentlemen' about her: some showy chairs and a sofa (a sofa by all means): half a dozen prints in gilt frames hanging up: some swinging book-shelves with novels and tracts upon them: a dinner brought in by a girl that is perhaps better 'educated' than she: two or three nick-nacks to eat instead of a piece of bacon and a pudding: the house too neat for a dirty-shoed carter to be allowed to come into; and every thing proclaiming to every sensible beholder, that there is here a constant anxiety to make a show not warranted by the reality. The children (which is the worst part of it) are all too clever to work: they are all to be gentlefolks. Go to plough! Good God! What, 'young gentlemen' go to plough! They become clerks, or some skimmy-dish thing or other. They flee from the dirty work as cunning horses do from the bridle. What misery is all this!

WILLIAM COBBETT (1763-1835)
from Rural Rides, Reigate 20th October 1825

Market Day

INTO some of the shops you stepped from the pavement down, as it were, into a cave, the level of the shop being eight or ten inches below the street, while the first floor projected over the pavement quite to the edge of the kerb. To enter these shops it was necessary to stoop, and when you were inside there was barely room to turn round …

But mean as a metropolitan shopman might have thought the spot, the business done there was large, and, more than that, it was genuine. The trade of a country market-town, especially when that market-town dates from the earliest days of English history, is hereditary. It flows to the same store and to the same shop year after year, generation after generation, century after century. The farmer who walks into the saddler's here goes in because his father went there before him. His father went in because his father dealt there, and so on farther back than memory can trace. It might almost be said that whole villages go to particular shops. You may see the agricultural labourers' wives, for instance, on a Saturday leave the village in a bevy of ten or a dozen, and all march in to the same tradesman. Of course in these latter days speculative men and 'co-operative' prices, industriously placarded, have sapped and undermined this old-fashioned system. Yet even now it retains sufficient hold to be a marked feature of country life …

On a market-day like this there is, of course, the incessant entry and exit of carts, waggons, traps, gigs, four-wheels, and a large number of private carriages. The number of private carriages is, indeed, very remarkable, as also the succession of gentlemen on thoroughbred horses—a proof of the number of resident gentry in the neighbourhood, and of its general prosperity. Cart-horses furbished up for sale, with strawbound tails and glistening skins; 'baaing' flocks of sheep; squeaking pigs; bullocks with their heads held ominously low, some going, some returning, from the auction yard; shouting drovers; lads rushing hither and thither; dogs barking; everything and everybody crushing, jostling, pushing through the narrow street. An old shepherd, who had done his master's business, comes along the pavement, trudging thoughtful and slow, with ashen staff. One hand is in his pocket, the elbow of the arm projecting; he is feeling a fourpenny-piece, and deliberating at which 'tap' he shall spend it. He fills up the entire pavement, and stolidly plods on, turning ladies and all into the roadway; not from intentional rudeness, but from sheer inability to perceive that he is causing inconvenience.

RICHARD JEFFERIES (1848-1887)
from Hodge and his Masters

July

NAUGHT moves but clouds, and in the glassy lake
Their doubles and the shadow of my boat.
The boat itself stirs only when I break
This drowse of heat and solitude afloat
To prove if what I see be bird or mote,
Or learn if yet the shore woods be awake.

Long hours since dawn grew,—spread,—and passed on high
And deep below,—I have watched the cool reeds hung
Over images more cool in imaged sky:
Nothing there was worth thinking of so long;
All that the ring-doves say, far leaves among,
Brims my mind with content thus still to lie.

EDWARD THOMAS (1878-1917)

The Old Vicarage, Grantchester

JUST now the lilac is in bloom,
All before my little room;
And in my flower-beds, I think,
Smile the carnation and the pink;
And down the borders, well I know,
The poppy and the pansy blow ...
Oh! there the chestnuts, summer through,
Beside the river make for you
A tunnel of green gloom, and sleep
Deeply above; and green and deep
The stream mysterious glides beneath,
Green as a dream and deep as death.
—Oh, damn! I know it! and I know
How the May fields all golden show,
And when the day is young and sweet,
Gild gloriously the bare feet
That run to bathe ...

RUPERT BROOKE (1887-1915)

An Ancient Sea

WHERE I live the wells are over ninety feet deep, at which depth in some dim age the sea once rolled. This I know, for when a few years since I was engaged in cleaning out a disused well, and in order to do this effectually caused it to be deepened by a few feet, we came upon sea sand containing many thousands of shells, all of them common and familiar to us today. It was curious to look at them and wonder how many ages had gone by since they were washed to the lip of the tide and left there by the retreating waves. Very many, I suppose, for ninety feet of clay and other substances take a long time to deposit. But whenever it was, the climate was the climate of England as we know it, for had it been either tropical or arctic the shells would have differed in character.

RIDER HAGGARD (1856-1925)
from A Farmer's Year

Nature is Company Enough

ONE of the pleasantest things in the world is going a journey; but I like to go by myself. I can enjoy society in a room; but out of doors, Nature is company enough for me. I am then never less alone than when alone.

I cannot see the wit of walking and talking at the same line. When I am in the country I wish to vegetate like the country. I am not for criticising hedge-rows and black cattle. I go out of town in order to forget the town and all that is in it. There are those who for this purpose go to watering-places, and carry the metropolis with them. I like more elbow-room and fewer encumbrances. I like solitude, when I give myself up to it, for the sake of solitude; nor do I ask for 'A friend in my retreat, Whom I may whisper solitude is sweet.'

The soul of a journey is liberty, perfect liberty, to think, feel, do, just as one pleases. We go a journey chiefly to be free of all impediments and of all inconveniences; to leave ourselves behind, much more than to get rid of others. It is because I want a little breathing-space to muse on indifferent matters … that I absent myself from the town for a while, without feeling at a loss the moment I am left by myself. Instead of a friend in a post-chaise or in a Tilbury, to exchange good things with, and vary the same stale topics over again, for once let me have a truce with impertinence. Give me the clear blue sky over my head, and the green turf beneath my feet, a winding road before me, and a three-hours march to dinne—and then to thinking! It is hard if I cannot start some game on these lone heaths. I laugh, I run, I leap, I sing for joy. From the point of yonder rolling cloud I plunge into my past being, and revel there, as the sun-burnt Indian plunges headlong into the wave that wafts him to his native shore …

WILLIAM HAZLITT (1778-1830)
from On Going a Journey

Golden Brown

BESIDE her were two young women, both in the freshness of youth and health. Their faces glowed with a golden-brown, and so great is the effect of colour that their plain features were transfigured. The sunlight under their faces made them beautiful. The summer light had been absorbed by the skin and now shone forth from it again; as certain substances exposed to the day absorb light and emit a phosphorescent gleam in the darkness of night, so the sunlight had been drunk up by the surface of the skin, and emanated from it.

Hour after hour in the gardens and orchards they worked in the full beams of the sun, gathering fruit for the London market, resting at midday in the shade of the elms in the corner. Even then they were in the sunshine—even in the shade, for the air carries it, or its influence, as it carries the perfumes of flowers ... There was that in their cheeks that all the wealth of London could not purchase—a superb health in their carriage princesses could not obtain ... Beautiful golden-brown in their cheeks, superb health in their gait, they walked as the Immortals on earth ... If so they chose, and without stress or strain, they could see the sun rise, they could be with him as it were—unwearied and without distress—the livelong day; they could stay on while the moon rose over the corn, and till the silent stars at silent midnight shone in the cool summer night, and on and on till the cock crew and the faint dawn appeared...

RICHARD JEFFERIES (1848-1887)
from The Open Air

In Hilly-Wood

HOW sweet to be thus nestling deep in boughs,
   Upon an ashen stoven pillowing me;
Faintly are heard the ploughmen at their ploughs,
   But not an eye can find its way to see.
The sunbeams scarce molest me with a smile,
   So thick the leafy armies gather round;
And where they do, the breeze blows cool the while,
   Their leafy shadows dancing on the ground.
Full many a flower, too, wishing to be seen,
Perks up its head the hiding grass between.—
In mid-wood silence, thus, how sweet to be;
   Where all the noises, that on peace intrude,
Come from the chittering cricket, bird, and bee,
   Whose songs have charms to sweeten solitude.

JOHN CLARE (1793-1864)

Tree Felling

TIMBER-felling, where the trees are at all crowded, is an operation that requires great skill and judgment. The first thing the woodman must do is to decide in which direction the trunk is to fall and the exact spot of ground whereon he desires to lay it … He places his ladder against the trunk, and, climbing as high as he can go, so that there may be a better pull and purchase at the moment of the fall, ties his line about the tree. Then he goes to a distance and makes the other end of the line, which is about thirty yards long, fast to the bole of a second tree … Should there be no tree near of sufficient strength to bear the strain, then at the critical moment the line must be held by men … The object of this rope is to make it sure that in spite of other precautions the tree will not fall in a direction different to that intended, thereby causing damage, or possibly hurt, to the woodcutters; for should it begin to fall thus perversely, the slack comes out of the rope, which, growing taut and rigid as a bar of iron when it takes the strain, swings the dead weight of the trunk round and brings it to the earth near to the place where it is desired that it should lie …

Then the actual felling begins. This there are two ways of doing—one the careless and slovenly chopping off of the tree above the level of the ground, the other its scientific 'rooting'. In rooting a timber, the soil is first removed from about the foot of the bole till the great roots are discovered branching this way and that. Then the woodmen begin upon these with their mattocks, which sink with a dull thud into the soft and sappy fibre, first cutting those of them that are upon the rope side, leaving only the great tap-root … Then they begin upon the bole, cutting it with hundreds of strokes, none of them delivered with very great force, and to the eye of the careless observer apparently aimed at random, which ends in shaping it to the form of a pear, the stalk of the pear being represented by the tap-root and the portion of timber that still remains above …

When the cutting has gone so deep that the shape of the bole approaches to that of a peg-top, the woodmen go to the end of the rope and pull upon it. Probably the tree makes no sign, but, with the exception of an occasional slight quiver as though of fear, which causes the twigs to tremble to their tips, stands as proud and upright as it has stood for the last century or more. Thereupon one of the men remarks to his mate that 'she wants a chip or two off the hinder side', and then comes another five minutes of quiet and scientific chopping, followed by a return to the end of the rope. At about the third tug the observer will notice the topmost twigs of timber bend themselves with a sudden curve, not unlike that of the top joint of a rod when a trout first takes the fly. At the next pull the curve is more sudden, and deeper. Now the great tree begins to groan and rock, and its boughs, rushing to and fro, to flog the air in wide sweeps, but still with a desperate tenacity the thin neck of wood and the remaining rope of root keep it from falling.

'She's a-coming,' says the head woodman; now togither, lad, togither.' Two more pulls and the doomed tree swings so far that it cannot recover its upright position. For a moment it hangs trembling, as though making obeisance to its murderers; then— a swift rush, a sound of wood rending and of tough roots flying apart with a noise like that of pistol shots, and down it tumbles to the earth with a thunderous rattling crash that echoes through the wood and dies far away upon the breast of the quiet river.

It is done, and a change has come over the landscape; the space that for generations has been filled with leafy branches is now white and empty air.

RIDER HAGGARD (1856-1925)
from A Farmer's Year

The Village Blacksmith

THE blacksmith, of course, is there—sometimes more than one —usually with plenty to do; for modern agriculture uses three times as much machinery and ironwork as was formerly the case. At first the blacksmiths did not understand how to mend many of these new-fangled machines, but they have learned a good deal, though some of the pieces still have to be replaced from the implement factories if broken. Horses come trooping in to have new shoes put on. Sometimes a village blacksmith acquires a fame for shoeing horses which extends far beyond his forge, and gentlemen residing in the market-towns send out their horses to him to be shod. He still uses a ground-ash sapling to hold the short chisel with which he cuts off the glowing iron on the anvil. He keeps bundles of the young, pliant ground-ash sticks, which twist easily and are peculiarly tough; and taking one of these, with a few turns of his wrist winds it round the chisel so as to have a long handle. One advantage of the wood is that it 'gives' a little, and does not jar when struck.

RICHARD JEFFERIES (1848-1887)
from Wild Life in a Southern County

A Boy's Song

WHERE the pools are bright and deep,
Where the grey trout lies asleep,
Up the river and o'er the lea,
That's the way for Billy and me.

Where the blackbird sings the latest,
Where the hawthorn blooms the sweetest,
Where the nestlings chirp and flee,
That's the way for Billy and me.

Where the mowers mow the cleanest,
Where the hay lies thick and greenest;
There to trace the homeward bee,
That's the way for Billy and me.

Where the hazel bank is steepest,
Where the shadow falls the deepest,
Where the clustering nuts fall free,
That's the way for Billy and me …

But this I know, I love to play
Through the meadow, among the hay:
Up the water and o'er the lea,
That's the way for Billy and me.

JAMES HOGG (1770-1835)

Run Hard, Fox

SUDDENLY a pheasant is hurled out of a neighbouring copse; something crosses the road; and out over a large and shining meadow goes a fox, tall and red, going easily as if he sailed in the wind. He crosses that meadow, then another, and he is half a mile away before a loud halloo sounds in the third field, and a mile away before the first hound crosses the road upon his scent.

Run hard, hounds, and drown the jackdaws' calling with your concerted voices. It is good to see your long swift train across the meadow and away, away; on such a day a man would give everything to run like that. Run hard, fox, and may you escape, for it would not be well to die on such a day, unless you could perchance first set your fair teeth into the throats of the foolish ones who now break through the hedge on great horses and pursue you—I know not why—ignorant of the command that has gone forth from the heart of this high blue heaven, Be beautiful and enjoy and live!

EDWARD THOMAS (1878-1917)
from The Heart of England

The Combe

THE combe was ever dark, ancient and dark.
Its mouth is stopped with bramble, thorn, and briar;
And no one scrambles over the sliding chalk
By beech and yew and perishing juniper
Down the half precipices of its sides, with roots
And rabbit holes for steps. The sun of winter,
The moon of summer, and all the singing birds
Except the missel-thrush that loves juniper,
Are quite shut out. But far more ancient and dark
The combe looks since they killed the badger there,
Dug him out and gave him to the hounds,
That most ancient Briton of English beasts.

EDWARD THOMAS (1878-1917)

August

ACROSS the gap made by our English hinds,
Amidst the Roman's handiwork, behold
Far off the long-roofed church; the shepherd binds
The withy round the hurdles of his fold;
Down in the foss the river fed of old,
That through long lapse of time has grown to be
The little grassy valley that you see.

Rest here awhile, not yet the eve is still,
The bees are wandering yet, and you may hear
The barley mowers on the trenchèd hill,
The sheep-bells, and the restless changing weir,
All little sounds made musical and clear
Beneath the sky that burning August gives,
While yet the thought of glorious Summer lives.

WILLIAM MORRIS (1834-1896)

The Exuberant Rooks

THE evening proceedings and manoeuvres of the rooks are curious and amusing in the autumn. Just before dusk they return in long strings from the foraging of the day, and rendezvous by thousands over Selborne down, where they wheel round in the air, and sport and dive in a playful manner, all the while exerting their voices, and making a loud cawing, which, being blended and softened by the distance that we at the village are below them, becomes a confused noise or chiding; or rather a pleasing murmur, very engaging to the imagination, and not unlike the cry of a pack of hounds in hollow, echoing woods, or the rushing of the wind in tall trees, or the tumbling of the tide upon a pebbly shore. When this ceremony is over, with the last gleam of day, they retire for the night to the deep beechen woods of Tisted and Ropley. We remember a little girl who, as she was going to bed, used to remark on such an occurrence, in the true spirit of physico-theology, that the rooks were saying their prayers; and yet this child was much too young to be aware that the Scriptures have said of the Deity—that 'he feedeth the ravens who call upon him.'

GILBERT WHITE (1720-1793)
From The Natural History of Selborne

Going to the Pub

IT is odd enough how differently one is affected by the same sight, under different circumstances. At the 'Holly-Bush' at Headley there was a room full of fellows in white smock frocks, drinking and smoking and talking, and I, who was then dry and warm, moralized within myself on their folly in spending their time in such a way. But, when I got down from Hindhead to the public-house at Road-Lane, with my skin soaking and my teeth chattering, I thought just such another group, whom I saw through the window sitting round a good fire with pipes in their mouths, the wisest assembly I had ever set my eyes on. A real Collective Wisdom. And, I most solemnly declare, that I felt a greater veneration for them than I have ever felt even for the Privy Council.

WILLIAM COBBETT (1763-1835)
from Rural Rides

The New Reaper

THIS morning we set the new reaper to work on the glebe fields of oats, which are bearing a good crop for so scaldy a piece of land, owing doubtless to the wet of the early summer. Before the machine can be put in, a pathway for it must be mown round the field with a scythe. Then the thing starts, drawn by two horses. It is beautiful to see it work, for it cuts wonderfully clean, the arms sweeping the bundles of corn from the platform in sheaves, ready for the binder. By a clever contrivance of the mechanism, this act is not always performed by the same arm. The limb that at one revolution delivers the bundle from the table to the ground, at the next merely bends the straw over the knives, while another dips down to the platform and clears it.

Thus into these various and complex operations the strength of the horses is transformed and distributed to each of them in such proportion as is needful. Care, however, must be taken at the corners, where the reaper turns, or it will jam; indeed, it is well for a man to round these off with a scythe. Some people yoke three horses to such machines, but I use only two, which are changed at noon, as half a day's work with a reaper behind them is quite enough for a pair of horses.

RIDER HAGGARD (1856-1925)
from A Farmer's Year

Autumn

I LOVE the fitful gust that shakes
  The casement all the day,
And from the mossy elm tree takes
  The faded leaf away,
Twirling it by the window pane
With thousand others down the lane.

I love to see the shaking twig
  Dance till the shut of eve,
The sparrow on the cottage rig,
  Whose chirp would make believe
That spring was just now flirting by
In summer's lap with flowers to lie.

I love to see the cottage smoke
  Curl upwards through the trees;
The pigeons nestled round the cote
  On November days like these;
The cock upon the dunghill crowing,
The mill sails on the heath a-going …

JOHN CLARE (1793-1864)

To Autumn

SEASON of mists and mellow fruitfulness,
    Close bosom-friend of the maturing sun;
Conspiring with him how to load and bless
    With fruit the vines that round the thatch-eaves run;
To bend with apples the mossed cottage-trees,
    And fill all fruit with ripeness to the core;
      To swell the gourd, and plump the hazel shells
    With a sweet kernel; to set budding more,
And still more, later flowers for the bees,
Until they think warm days will never cease;
      For Summer has o'erbrimmed their clammy cells.

Who hath not seen thee oft amid thy store?
    Sometimes whoever seeks abroad may find
Thee sitting careless on a granary floor,
    Thy hair soft-lifted by the winnowing wind;
Or on a half-reaped furrow sound asleep,
    Drowsed with the fume of poppies, while thy hook
      Spares the next swath and all its twinèd flowers;
And sometimes like a gleaner thou dost keep
    Steady thy laden head across a brook;
    Or by a cider-press, with patient look,
      Thou watchest the last oozings, hours by hours.

Where are the songs of Spring? Ay, where are they?
　　Think not of them,—thou hast thy music too,
While barrèd clouds bloom the soft-dying day
　　And touch the stubble-plains with rosy hue;
Then in a wailful choir the small gnats mourn
　　Among the river sallows, borne aloft
　　　　Or sinking as the light wind lives or dies;
And full-grown lambs loud bleat from hilly bourn;
　　Hedge-crickets sing, and now with treble soft
　　The redbreast whistles from a garden-croft,
　　　　And gathering swallows twitter in the skies.

JOHN KEATS (1795-1821)

Quid Quo Pro

THIS great squire—he was a very rich, influential man—sent for me to go down to his house when my work was over, in order to canvass me. I went down, and after some talk he said to me, 'Do your Liberals find you employment?' 'What has that to do with my vote?' I said. 'I sell you my labour, but not my conscience; that's not for sale.'

'Oh!' said this big, strapping, six-foot man.

'Now look here, sir,' I said; 'I sat second horse behind you for several years, and I have worked in your stables, but since I have been out of your stables have you ever given me a sovereign without my having given you a sovereign's worth of good labour? No! You know I have always given you a sovereign's worth of labour for every sovereign you have given me, and therefore why should I give you my vote because I sell you my labour?'

'Then,' said he, 'Sit down, Joe, and have a glass of sherry.'

JOSEPH ARCH (1826-1919)
from The Story of His Life, Told by himself, 1898

A Point of View

PEOPLE who live amidst fine scenery are apt to treat it with contempt, partly from familiarity and partly (I think) because they do not see the scenery as other people see it. You form a higher opinion of a man if you have only seen him at his best, than if you have also seen him at his worst and in all intermediate states. It is the same with scenery. Most strangers see this district [Lustleigh, Devon] in the height of summer, whereas the native see it in the winter time as well, and have both aspects of it in their mind when they are looking at it; and they sometimes show impatience when strangers praise it overmuch. A farmer here was leaning over a gate from which there is a glorious view. Seeing the view, a passer-by remarked to him how glorious it was. The farmer answered, 'Durn the view. I bain't lookin' at no view. I be lookin' how they dratted rabbits 'as ated up my tunnips.'

CECIL TORR (1857-1928)
from Small Talk at Wreyland

To a Young Lady on her Leaving the Town

… SHE went to plain-work, and to purling brooks,
Old-fashioned halls, dull aunts, and croaking rooks;
She went from Opera, Park, Assembly, Play,
To morning walks, and prayers three hours a day;
To part her time 'twixt reading and bohea,
To muse, and spill her solitary tea,
Or o'er cold coffee trifle with the spoon,
Count the slow clock, and dine exact at noon;
Divert her eyes with pictures in the fire,
Hum half a tune, tell stories to the Squire;
Up to her godly garret after seven,
There starve and pray, for that's the way to Heaven.

Some Squire, perhaps, you take delight to rack,
Whose game is whist, whose treat a toast in sack;
Who visits with a gun, presents you birds,
Then gives a smacking buss, and cries: 'No words!'
Or with his hound comes hallooing from the stable,
Makes love with nods and knees beneath a table;
Whose laughs are hearty, though his jests are coarse,
And loves you best of all things—but his horse …

ALEXANDER POPE (1688-1744)

Solitude

HAPPY the man, whose wish and care
A few paternal acres bound,
Content to breathe his native air
    In his own ground.

Whose herds with milk, whose fields with bread,
Whose flocks supply him with attire;
Whose trees in summer yield him shade,
    In winter fire.

Blest, who can unconcernedly find
Hours, days, and years, slide soft away
In health of body, peace of mind,
    Quiet by day,

Sound sleep by night; study and ease
Together mixed, sweet recreation,
And innocence, which most does please
    With meditation.

Thus let me live, unseen, unknown;
Thus unlamented let me die;
Steal from the world, and not a stone
    Tell where I lie.

ALEXANDER POPE (1688-1744)

November

THE mellow year is hastening to its close;
The little birds have almost sung their last,
Their small notes twitter in the dreary blast—
That shrill-piped harbinger of early snows;
The patient beauty of the scentless rose,
Oft with the morn's hoar crystal quaintly glassed
Hangs, a pale mourner for the summer past,
And makes a little summer where it grows;
In the chill sunbeam of the faint brief day
The dusky waters shudder as they shine,
The russet leaves obstruct the straggling way
Of oozy brooks, which no deep banks define,
And the gaunt woods, in ragged, scant array,
Wrap their old limbs with sombre ivy twine.

HARTLEY COLERIDGE (1796-1849)

Hacking Turnips in the Rain

THE swede-field in which she [Tess] and her companion were set hacking was a stretch of a hundred odd acres, in one patch, on the highest ground of the farm, rising above stony lanchets or lynchets … The upper half of each turnip had been eaten off by the live-stock, and it was the business of the two women to grub up the lower or earthy half of the root with a hooked fork called a hacker, that it might be eaten also …

Nobody came near them, and their movements showed a mechanical regularity; their forms standing enshrouded in hessian 'wroppers'—sleeved brown pinafores, tied behind to the bottom, to keep their gowns from blowing about—scant skirts revealing boots that reached high up the ankles, and yellow sheepskin gloves with gauntlets …

They worked on hour after hour, unconscious of the forlorn aspect they bore in the landscape, not thinking of the justice or injustice of their lot. Even in such a position as theirs it was possible to exist in a dream. In the afternoon the rain came on again, and Marian said that they need not work any more. But if they did not work they would not be paid; so they worked on. It was so high a situation, this field, that the rain had no occasion to fall, but raced along horizontally upon the yelling wind, sticking into them like glass splinters till they were wet through. Tess had not known till now what was really meant by that. There are degrees of dampness, and a very little is called being wet through in common talk. But to stand working slowly in a field, and feel the creep of rain-water, first in legs and shoulders, then on hips and head, then at back, front, and sides, and yet to work on till the leaden light diminishes and marks that the sun is down, demands a distinct modicum of stoicism, even of valour.

THOMAS HARDY (1840-1928)
from Tess of the D'Urbervilles

Winter

THE frost is here,
And fuel is dear,
And woods are sear,
And fires burn clear,
And frost is here
And has bitten the heel of the going year.

Bite, frost, bite!
You roll up away from the light
The blue wood-louse and the plump doormouse,
And the bees are stilled, and the flies are killed,
And you bite far into the heart of the house,
But not into mine.

Bite, frost, bite!
The woods are all the searer,
The fuel is all the dearer,
The fires are all the clearer,
My spring is all the nearer,
You have bitten into the heart of the earth
But not into mine.

ALFRED, LORD TENNYSON (1809-1892)

Frost at Midnight

THE Frost performs its secret ministry,
Unhelped by any wind. The owlet's cry
Came loud—and hark, again! loud as before.
The inmates of my cottage, all at rest,
Have left me to that solitude, which suits
Abstruser musings: save that at my side
My cradled infant slumbers peacefully …
                For I was reared
In the great city, pent 'mid cloisters dim,
And saw nought lovely but the sky and stars.
But thou, my babe! shalt wander like a breeze
By lakes and sandy shores, beneath the crags
Of ancient mountain, and beneath the clouds,
Which image in their bulk both lakes and shores
And mountain crags: so shalt thou see and hear
The lovely shapes and sounds intelligible
Of that eternal language, which thy God
Utters, who from eternity doth teach
Himself in all, and all things in himself.
Great universal Teacher! he shall mould
Thy spirit, and by giving make it ask.

Therefore all seasons shall be sweet to thee,
Whether the summer clothe the general earth
With greenness, or the redbreast sit and sing

Betwixt the tufts of snow on the bare branch
Of mossy apple-tree, while the nigh thatch
Smokes in the sun-thaw; whether the eave-drops fall
Heard only in the trances of the blast,
Or if the secret ministry of frost
Shall hang them up in silent icicles,
Quietly shining to the quiet Moon.

SAMUEL TAYLOR COLERIDGE (1772-1834)

III

The Darkling Thrush

I LEANT upon a coppice gate
    When Frost was spectre-grey,
And Winter's dregs made desolate
    The weakening eye of day.
The tangled bine-stems scored the sky
    Like strings of broken lyres,
And all mankind that haunted nigh
    Had sought their household fires.

The land's sharp features seemed to be
    The Century's corpse outleant,
His crypt the cloudy canopy,
    The wind his death-lament.
The ancient pulse of germ and birth
    Was shrunken hard and dry,
And every spirit upon earth
    Seemed fervourless as I.

At once a voice burst forth among
    The bleak twigs overhead
In a full-hearted evensong
    Of joy illimited;
And aged thrush, frail, gaunt and small,
    In blast-beruffled plume,
Had chosen thus to fling his soul
    Upon the growing gloom.

So little cause for carolings
   Of such ecstatic sound
Was written on terrestrial things
   Afar or nigh around,
That I could think there trembled through
   His happy good-night air
Some blessed hope, whereof he knew
   And I was unaware.

THOMAS HARDY (1840-1928)

Snow

7 January, 1776. SNOW driving all the day, which was followed by frost, sleet, and some snow, till the twelfth, when a prodigious mass overwhelmed all the works of man …

On the fourteenth the writer was obliged to be much abroad, and thinks he never before or since encountered such rugged, Siberian weather. Many of the narrow roads are now filled above the tops of the hedges, through which the snow was driven in most romantic and grotesque shapes, so striking to the imagination as not to be seen without wonder and pleasure. The poultry dared not stir out of their roosting-places, for cocks and hens are so dazzled and confounded by the glare of the snow that they would soon perish without assistance. The hares also lay sullenly in their seats, and would not move till compelled by hunger, being conscious, poor animals, that the drifts and heaps treacherously betray their footsteps, and prove fatal to numbers of them …

All this time the cold was not very intense, for the thermometer stood at 29, 28, 25, and thereabout; but on the twenty-first it descended to 20. The birds now began to be in a very pitiable and starving condition. Tamed by the season, skylarks settled in the streets of towns, because they saw the ground was bare; rooks frequented dunghills close to houses; and crows watched horses as they passed, and greedily devoured what dropped from them …

GILBERT WHITE (1720-1793)
Letter to the Hon Daines Barrington

Lines for a Bed at Kelmscott Manor

THE wind's on the wold
And the night is a-cold,
And Thames runs chill
'Twixt mead and hill,
But kind and dear
Is the old house here,
And my heart is warm,
Midst winter's harm.
Rest then and rest,
And think of the best
'Twixt summer and spring
When all birds sing
In the town of the tree,
And ye lie in me
And scarce dare move
Lest earth and its love
Should fade away
Ere the full of the day.

I am old and have seen
Many things that have been,
Both grief and peace,
And wane and increase.
No tale I tell
Of ill or well,

But this I say,
Night treadeth on day,
And for worst and best
Right good is rest.

WILLIAM MORRIS (1834-1896)

Snow

IT sifts from Leaden Sieves—
It powders all the Wood
It fills with Alabaster Wool
The Wrinkles of the Road—

It makes an Even Face
Of Mountain, and of Plain—
Unbroken Forehead from the East
Unto the East again—

It reaches to the Fence—
It wraps it Rail by Rail
Till it is lost in Fleeces—
It deals Celestial Vail

To Stump, and Stack—and Stem—
A Summer's empty Room—
Acres of Joints, where Harvests were,
Recordless, but for them—

It Ruffles Wrists of Posts
As Ankles of a Queen—
Then stills its Artisans—like Ghosts—
Denying they have been—

EMILY DICKINSON (1830-1886)

Liberty

MY sister Emily loved the moors. Flowers brighter than the rose bloomed in the blackest of the heath for her; out of a sullen hollow in a livid hill-side her mind could make an Eden. She found in the bleak solitude many and dear delights; and not the least and best loved was—liberty.

Liberty was the breath of Emily's nostrils; without it, she perished. The change from her own home to a school, and from her own very noiseless, very secluded, but unrestricted and inartificial mode of life, to one of disciplined routine (though under the kindliest auspices), was what she failed in enduring. Her nature proved here too strong for her fortitude. Every morning when she woke, the vision of home and the moors rushed on her, and darkened and saddened the day that lay before her. Nobody knew what ailed her but me—I knew only too well. In this struggle her health was quickly broken: her white face, attenuated form, and failing strength, threatened rapid decline … She was never happy till she carried her hard-won knowledge back to the remote English village, the old parsonage house, and desolate Yorkshire hills. A very few years more, and she looked her last on those hills, and breathed her last in that house, and under the aisle of that obscure village church found her last lowly resting-place. Merciful was the decree that spared her when she was a stranger in a strange land, and guarded her dying bed with kindred love and congenial constancy.

CHARLOTTE BRONTË (1816-1855)

A Sense Sublime

FOR I have learned
To look on nature, not as in the hour
Of thoughtless youth; but hearing oftentimes
The still, sad music of humanity,
Nor harsh nor grating, though of ample power
To chasten and subdue. And I have felt
A presence that disturbs me with the joy
Of elevated thoughts; a sense sublime
Of something far more deeply interfused,
Whose dwelling is the light of setting suns,
And the round ocean and the living air,
And the blue sky, and in the mind of man:
A motion and a spirit, that impels
All thinking things, all objects of all thought,
And rolls through all things. Therefore am I still
A lover of the meadows and the woods,
And mountains; and of all that we behold
From this green earth; of all the mighty world
Of eye, and ear,—both what they half create,
And what perceive; well pleased to recognise
In nature and the language of the sense
The anchor of my purest thoughts, the nurse,
The guide, the guardian of my heart, and soul
Of all my moral being.

WILLIAM WORDSWORTH (1770-1850)
from Tintern Abbey

P.79
p 99